YOU'RE THE HERO
JUNGLE
ADVENTURE

Lily Murray
Illustrated by Essi Kimpimäki

IVY KIDS

CREATE YOUR OWN JUNGLE STORY!

WELCOME HERO!

This book will help you create a jungle adventure story — and you're the main character! Here's how it works:

1

Read the question at the top of the page. You'll be asked to make a choice.

2

Look at the pictures and decide what you'd like to add to your story.

You're about to go on an adventure. Which one of these heroes do you want to be?

A granny

A butterfly

A tourist

A scientist

A merman

A jaguar

An explorer

A treasure seeker

Remember — you're the hero! Add as many extra details as you want to shape your story. Tell it in your head, or read aloud as you go.

Once you're finished, go back to the start and see what happens when you make different choices. How many stories can you tell?

Or you can use this book however you want to tell a story. Your mission is to have as much fun as possible!

3
Read this part to get ready for the next bit of the adventure.

A jungle baby

A monkey

A princess

A snake

A photographer

A writer

A nature expert

A mini adventurer

Turn the page to pick some things to get dressed up in.

GOOD LUCK!
I'm coming too! Spot me hiding through the book.

You're about to go on an adventure. Which one of these heroes do you want to be?

A butterfly

A granny

A tourist

A scientist

A jaguar

A merman

An explorer

A treasure seeker

A jungle baby

A monkey

A princess

A snake

A photographer

A writer

A nature
expert

A mini
adventurer

Turn the page to pick some
things to get dressed up in.

What do you want to get dressed up in? Choose as many items as you like.

Fairy wings

A bushy beard

A poncho

Walking boots

A fruity headdress

A feather boa

A cap

A mask

Rollerblades

A belt

A safari hat

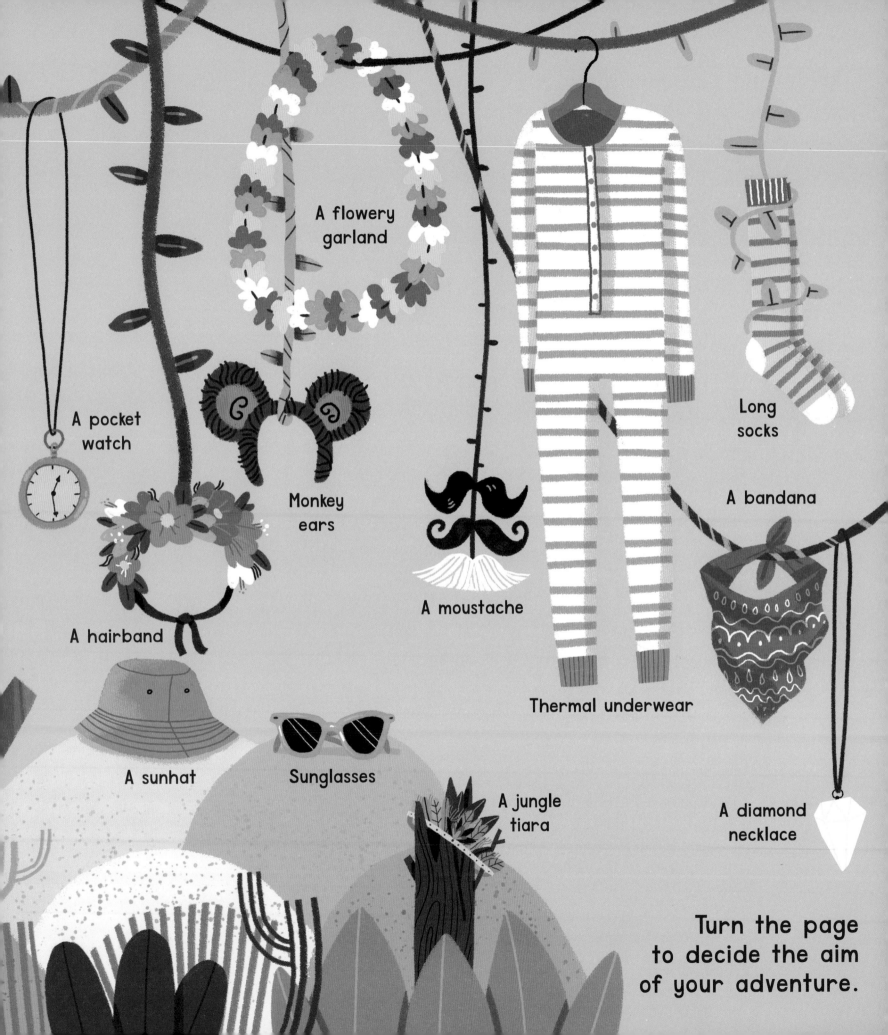

A flowery garland

A pocket watch

Monkey ears

A moustache

Long socks

A bandana

A hairband

Thermal underwear

A sunhat

Sunglasses

A jungle tiara

A diamond necklace

Turn the page to decide the aim of your adventure.

Why are you exploring the jungle? Pick a reason.

To swim in the jungle river

To peek at tiny elephants

To climb the tallest tree in the jungle

To travel to the City of Gold

To swing with monkeys

To peer into the Pool of Truth

To discover giant bugs

To find gems
and jewels

To look for cave paintings

To try tasty
jungle fruits

To search for
hidden treasure

To meet the
Jungle Prince

To find a fire-
breathing snake

To visit the fried egg mines

To go inside the largest
underground cave in the world

To see a flower that blooms
once every 100 years

Now you know what you're going to do,
it's time to pack your bag! Turn the
page to choose what to take.

What will you need in the jungle? You have room in your bag for three items.

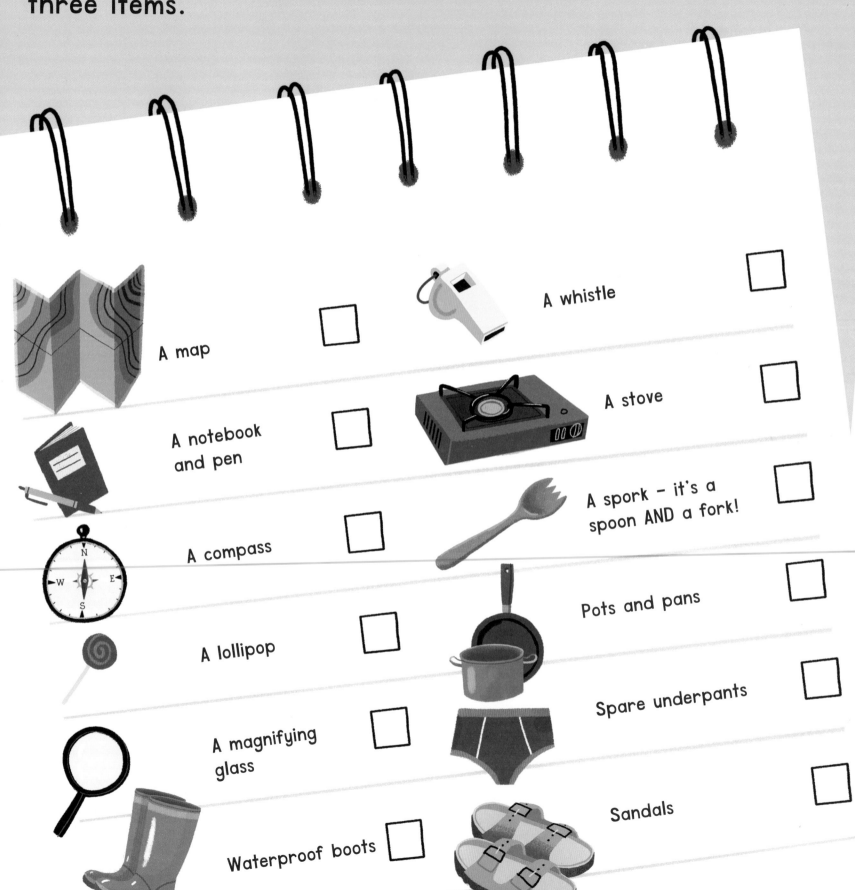

A map ☐

A notebook and pen ☐

A compass ☐

A lollipop ☐

A magnifying glass ☐

Waterproof boots ☐

A whistle ☐

A stove ☐

A spork – it's a spoon AND a fork! ☐

Pots and pans ☐

Spare underpants ☐

Sandals ☐

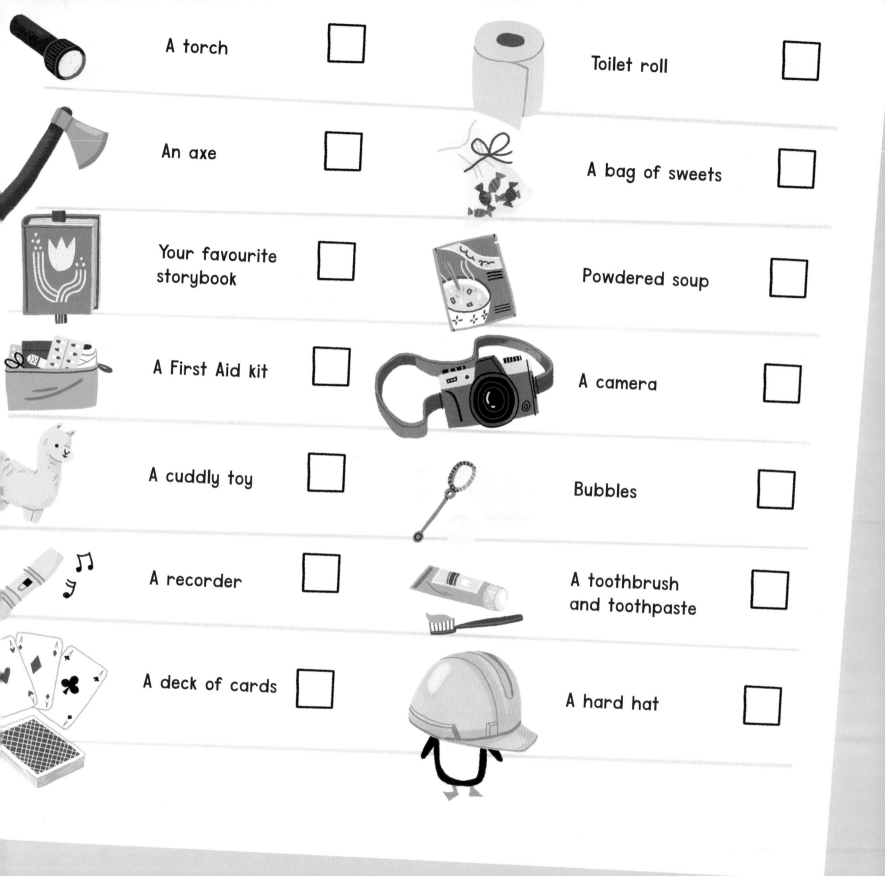

A torch ☐

Toilet roll ☐

An axe ☐

A bag of sweets ☐

Your favourite storybook ☐

Powdered soup ☐

A First Aid kit ☐

A camera ☐

A cuddly toy ☐

Bubbles ☐

A recorder ☐

A toothbrush and toothpaste ☐

A deck of cards ☐

A hard hat ☐

It could get lonely in the jungle...
Turn the page to choose a crew.

Do you want anyone to travel with you through the jungle? Choose as many crew members as you like.

A sloth

A jungle detective

A cook

A parrot

A snake tamer

A gang of monkeys

A robot

No one
(you'll explore
the jungle alone)

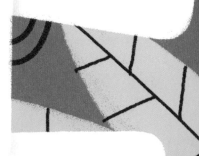

A survival
expert

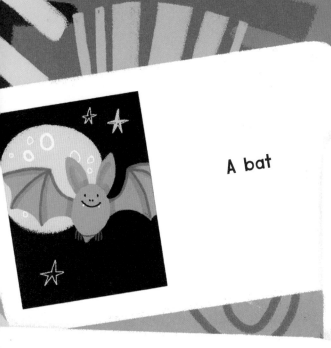

A bat

A dolphin

A bodybuilder

A doctor

A person
to carry
your bags

A fairy
queen

A band of
pocket-sized
people

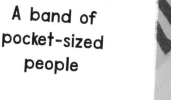

Time to get going! Turn the page
and decide how to travel in style.

How will you make your way through the jungle? Choose one way to get around.

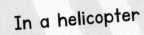
In a helicopter

You'll roll!

In a hot-air balloon

In an inflatable raft

You'll follow the elephants

In an off-road vehicle

You'll swim

You'll run with the jungle foxes

You'll swing from tree to tree

In a limo

You'll teleport

On a skateboard

In a plane

In a cable car

In a rowboat

In a speedboat

You're nearly ready to go. Turn the page to decide which path you'll take to get there.

Which one of these paths through the jungle will you take?

Across the treetop walkway

Over the waterfall

Around the volcano

Along the edge of the jungle

Past huge toadstools

Down the mines

Over the river

Through the thickest part of the jungle

Across the purple swamp

Between the
Mountains of Doom

Through the ruined city

Over the Lake
of Giant Crocs

Past the herd of
angry rhinos

Around
the jungle
village

Through
the veggie patch

Over hilltops

You have finally reached your destination. Is there someone waiting for you when you arrive? Turn the page to find out...

Yes, there's someone here to greet you! Who is it? Choose as many of them as you like.

A bear

A spider

A gold hunter

A one-man band

A puppy

A talking burger

An alien

A gorilla

WELCOME

Pixies

An acrobat

A friend from home

A horse

An invisible boy

A tiger

A librarian

An alligator

Thankfully, they're all friends and want to help you on your way. Turn the page and find a place to relax.

Where's your hero hangout?
Choose one.

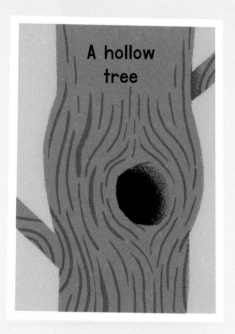
A hollow tree

A house on stilts

A tree house

An abandoned temple

A shelter made from leaves

A tent

A marsh

A hidden cottage

A mud hut

A hammock

A river barge

A bear's den

A nest

Roosting with bats

A camper van

A jungle hotel

You've found a place to chill. But don't get too cozy. There's danger just around the corner. Turn the page to find out more.

An enemy has appeared!
Who is it?

A bad fairy

A thirsty vampire bat

A hungry river monster

A wicked pirate

A crazy professor

A beastly King of the Apes

A grouchy jungle ogre

There's a way out! Which one will you choose?

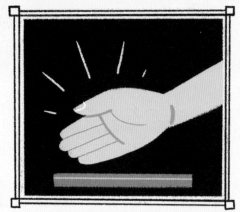

You karate-chop everything in sight until you're free

You sneak away through jungle tunnels

You call on the bugs of the forest to help you

You wish for a fairy godmother... she appears and rescues you!

You backflip your way out of trouble

You become super strong! The enemy is no match for you

You blow spit bubbles to distract your enemy and slip away

You run off with lightning speed

You swing through the trees to freedom

You confuse your enemy with a hypnotic jungle boogie!

You make a deal with your enemy by giving them sweets

You make an explosive from things in your bag and blast your way out

You disguise yourself as a sloth and crawl away

You had already set your own traps, and capture your enemy!

You agree to be friends with your enemy

You tickle your way out of trouble

You all escape! Over the page, pick a prize for being a great hero.

Which one of these things will you choose as your reward?

Tickets to the jungle funfair

Helpful fairies who'll follow you anywhere

A pedicure

A massive cake

A magic flute

Brand-new climbing gear

A rare plant

A bike

Amazing friends

The biggest gem in the world

A huge teddy

A crown

A mystery box... What's inside?

A trophy

A pet chameleon

Lots of money

Your adventure is nearly over. There's just one more choice to make on the next page...

What will happen next? Choose an ending for your tale.

JUNGLE NEWS

YOU SAIL HOME DOWN THE JUNGLE RIVER

YOU DECIDE TO BECOME... A PIRATE!

YOU GET STUCK IN A MINE!

YOU SEARCH FOR MAGICAL JUNGLE CREATURES!

A FIREWORK DISPLAY IS HELD IN YOUR HONOUR

YOU HEAD HOME TO CHILL

YOU FIND A JUNGLE TUNNEL TO EXPLORE

YOU TAKE A PART OF THE JUNGLE WITH YOU

YOU ADOPT A PET MONKEY

YOU RIDE OFF ON THE
BACK OF A ZEBRA

YOU FIND A TREASURE MAP

YOU SET UP A JUNGLE SCHOOL

YOU WRITE A BOOK ABOUT
YOUR ADVENTURE

YOU BUY YOUR VERY OWN
TROPICAL ISLAND

YOU DECIDE TO LIVE IN THE JUNGLE FOREVER

YOU BECOME FAMOUS

You've told a brilliant story. Good luck on all your future adventures!

First published in the UK in 2020 by

Ivy Kids

An imprint of The Quarto Group
The Old Brewery
6 Blundell Street
London N7 9BH
United Kingdom
www.QuartoKnows.com

British Library Cataloguing-in-Publication Data
A catalogue record for this book is available from the British Library.

ISBN: 978-1-78240-938-0

This book was conceived, designed & produced by

Ivy Kids

58 West Street, Brighton BN1 2RA, United Kingdom

PUBLISHER David Breuer
MANAGING EDITOR Susie Behar
COMMISSIONING EDITOR Lucy Menzies
ART DIRECTOR Hanri van Wyk
DESIGNER Kate Haynes
IN-HOUSE EDITOR Hannah Dove
EXTERNAL DESIGNER Emily Portnoi

Manufactured in Guangdong, China CC012020

1 3 5 7 9 10 8 6 4 2

MIX
Paper from
responsible sources
FSC
www.fsc.org FSC® C008047

THE END
Now go back to the start
and have another adventure!